THE QUIET LAND

THE QUIET LAND

James A. Warner

GROSSMAN PUBLISHERS

NEW YORK • 1970

Published by Grossman Publishers, Inc.
125A East 19th Street
New York, N. Y. 10003

Published simultaneously in Canada by
Fitzhenry and Whiteside, Ltd.

Manufactured in the United States.

Library of Congress Catalogue Card Number 76-121703

To my grandchildren

PENNY - PAM

FRANKIE

and their Grandmother

Acknowledgement is made

to

Beverley Stastny

who did the text and chose the poems

and quotations used.

Without her help this book would not have been possible.

Preface

Many people ask why I have chosen for my subjects the Plain People who live in and around Lancaster, Pennsylvania. These people have always fascinated me, with their quaint manner of dress and speech, their isolation and independence, and their strict adherence to their faith. The natural beauty of the countryside, where they live with its rolling hills, green valleys, old covered bridges and neat farmhouses all combine to make the area a color photographer's dream.

A general atmosphere of peace and serenity prevails in this countryside, a peace which allows me to escape, if only for a short time, the pressures and problems of the business world.

In the glow of the lanterns and firelight, the scene always reminds me of old-fashioned Christmas cards. This is one of the many scenes I keep in mind, hoping that some day I may capture on film one more fragment of the beauty and tranquillity of a world thought to be lost forever.

I love to sit in the corner of a barn at dusk, with the smell of hay in my nostrils, listening to the sparrows squabbling in the eaves overhead, watching the new-born calves and foals, awkward, yet charming.

It is a great pleasure to go out early in the morning and stand in a field of rustling corn; or watch the morning mist rise up through the trees in a meadow at dawn. It is so peaceful one can hear the distant song of a farmer drifting over the hills.

It is these moments of peace that draw me to the country of the Plain People of Pennsylvania.

When I go out photographing, I never decide beforehand to take a certain number of pictures that day. I go with the intent to relax and with the thought of hopefully capturing one memorable scene on film. There are times when I have driven home without taking a single picture, but my mind usually is full of many ideas for the next time.

As I drive along the backroads of the rural areas, I catch fleeting glimpses of many promising scenes which are not possible to photograph at that particular time. When I am able, I go back to the same spot, and if the light and general conditions are right, I try to recapture the mood of the scene as I remember it.

One crisp winter evening I saw a buggy full of youngsters pull into a side road which led to a frozen pond. It was a skating party and as they tumbled out of the buggy, the lanterns they carried lit their laughing rosy faces, giving them an ethereal quality strangely in keeping with the surroundings.

I sat in my car and watched as they trooped to the edge of the pond to build a bonfire. Soon several more buggies full of teenagers arrived to join in the fun of the marshmallow roast and skating. More fires were lit, and the orange-yellow flames roared in the ice cold air. Skittish and playful as yearling foals, the youngsters chased one another, pushing and dodging among the groups of marshmallow "cooks."

The Amish and related sects, have similar attitudes toward life. The close bonds created by these attitudes and beliefs unite the groups and at the same time isolate them from the outside world. Stemming from the conservative Old Order Amish are many other more liberal sects, each with its own varied forms of customs and worship.

Despite the differences, however, all are bound together by their traditions, basic beliefs and code of ethics. Their ideal is to live simple, work-filled lives, with humility and obedience to the word of God. Therefore when these people meet socially, they are accepted with love by one another as "Plain People."

Some of the more liberal groups do use modern conveniences, such as electricity and mechanized farm equipment. Others drive automobiles and enjoy radio and television. But never do they allow these "luxuries" to become the focal point of their lives. Their attitudes toward life in general, their thoughts and actions, are solidly molded by their religious beliefs. It could be said that they live their faith daily.

In the photographs I have tried to capture and project with affection my impression of the Plain People. I hope that I have contributed toward a closer understanding of these gentle people who live and work in the Quiet Land.

THE QUIET LAND

Around the child bend all the three
Sweet Graces - Faith, Hope, Charity.
Around the man bend other faces -
Pride, Envy, Malice are his graces.

Walter Savage Landor

*"She looketh well to the ways of
her household, and eateth not the bread
of idleness."*
Old Testament

Nothing can so poignantly evoke the
flavor of the receding past as
some remembered tune,
some melody that has caught up and
woven into its own unconscious fabric
the very color and fragrance
of a day gone by.
Alexander Woollcott

Know you what it is to be a child?
It is to be something far different
from the man of today.
It is to have a spirit get steaming from
the waters of baptism;
it is to believe in love,
to believe in loneliness,
to believe in belief;
it is to be so little that the elves can
reach to whisper in your ear;
it is to turn pumpkins into coaches,
and mice into horses,
lowness into loftiness,
and nothing into everything,
for each child has its fairy godmother
in its soul.

Frances Thompson

I shall remember candlelight
And the low fire burning
When the only sound was a quiet word
Or a book page turning.

Mildred Bowers Armstrong

Oh, the comfort, the inexpressible comfort of feeling safe with a person, having neither to weigh thought nor measure words, but pouring them all right out, just as they chaff and grain together; certain that a faithful hand will take and sift them, keep what is worth keeping, and then with the breath of kindness blow the rest away.

Dinah Mulock Craik

Time Is
Too Slow for those who Wait,
Too Swift for those who Fear,
Too Long for those who Grieve,
Too Short for those who Rejoice;
But for those who Love,
Time is eternity.

Henry Van Dyke

Alice! a childish story take
And with a gentle hand
Lay it where childhood's dreams
*   are twined*
in memory's mystic band,
Like pilgrim's withered wreathe
*   of flowers*
Plucked in a far-off land.

Lewis Carroll

But when the sun in all its state
Illumed the eastern skies,
She passed about the kitchen grate
And went to making pies.

James Aldrich

There are two ways of spreading light:
  to be
The candle or the mirror that reflects it.

Edith Wharton

God conceived the world that was poetry;
He formed it; that was sculpture;
He colored it; that was painting;
He peopled it with human beings;
 that was the grand, divine, eternal drama.

Charlotte Cushman

I have never let my schooling interfere with my education.

Mark Twain

All that we see or seem
Is but a dream within a dream.
Edgar Allan Poe

The lantern makes a spot of gold,
Alien to the dark and cold,
Burning steady as it can,
As if a warm, good part of man
Were left outside there in the night
To go on working giving light.

Robert P. Tristram Coffin

Your prayers shall be the murmur
Of grasses in the rain;
The song of woodland thrushes
That makes God glad again.

Fanny Stearns Davis

Sweet childish days that were as
long
As twenty days are now.

William Wordsworth

The dreams of childhood —
its beautiful airy fables;
its graceful, beautiful, humane,
impossible adornments of the world
beyond: so good to be believed in once,
so glad to be remembered
when outgrown.

Charles Dickens

And he gave it for his opinion,
that whoever could make two blades
of grass, to grow upon a spot
where only one grew before,
would deserve better of mankind,
and do more for his country than the
whole race of politicians put together.

Jonathan Swift

All things that love the sun are
   out of doors;
The sky rejoices in the morning's birth;
The grass is bright with raindrops
   on the moors
The hare is running races in her mirth.
                    William Wordsworth

The Plain People have settled not only in Pennsylvania but in many areas of the North American Continent. From Florida to Manitoba they follow the good land. Wherever they choose to settle, because of their shrewd judgment of land and their application of time honored methods of farming, they are always successful in producing above average crops and providing a comfortable living for their families.

One common bond of interest which helps to hold together the widely scattered communities is their newspaper, "The Budget." Published in Sugar Creek, Ohio, it enjoys nationwide distribution. The content is usually news such as "The last of the sweet potatoes are in" or "Next Sunday's services will be held at Eli Stolfur's place." Little social events are entered in a gossipy tone: "Fanny Zook visited her mother on Sunday," "Emily Fisher has a brand new buggy," or "Elam Kling fell and broke his arm last week."

One person, in a village, usually a woman, acts as scribe. She gathers all the local news for "The Budget." Recent births, deaths, and marriages are recorded along with many little items which to "Outsiders" would seem dull and trivial.

The state of the weather is of great interest to rural folk. Remarks such as "It rained here all last week" and "The creek on Amos Lap's farm has overflowed twice since last fall" are the usual reports. These little tid-bits are read with great enthusiasm, and "The Budget" is considered as interesting and welcome as a letter from a member of the family.

In pre-Freudian times the general concept held by the culture was that humanities' deeds were influenced by celestial forces beyond human control. Therefore individuals were not responsible for their actions. This belief was never a part of the Plain doctrine which gives credit to God for providing humankind with a conscience, and the brains to distinguish between right and wrong. This philosophical attitude in general enables them to accept more easily disappointment and sorrow. Believing in God's infallible and mysterious ways, defiance, resentment and tensions dissolve replaced with quiet resignation and calm acceptance of trouble.

One of the basic principles of the Plain faith requires them to show courage in the face of adversity, and to work to overcome a bad situation without complaint. An Amish friend of mine discovered that an old stone dam on his property had burst in sub-zero weather. Instead of being annoyed and resentful about the extra work this repair would entail, his attitude of acceptance allowed him to see the beauty of the scene.

He pointed to the flow of icy water spilling from the crack and said, "Jim, what a great picture that would make."

In many respects the Plain People seem to practice a very literal version of the Christian principle of equality. When I first became acquainted with these people I was mildly surprised to find myself being immediately addressed as "Jim." I was, in turn, expected to use Christian names when addressing my new friends. One can imagine what an "English" parent would say to a child if he dared address an adult in this fashion. But the Plain children do this automatically. The formality of "Uncle and Aunt" or "Mr. and Mrs." is never observed. The only exceptions to this are their parents and grandparents.

These people are also free of much of the long established social etiquette that is second nature to us. One evening while I was visiting an Amish family, a man accidentally bumped into me as he passed by, but he did not pardon himself. His wife noticed this, and spoke to him in "Dutch"; whereupon he came to me, smiled, and said, "Jim, I didn't feel the need to apologize to you just now, because you know I didn't mean to bump into you." Their understanding of the concept of equality and their unquestioning confidence in the other person's honest intentions, render the traffic rules of etiquette unnecessary. They seem to give others credit for having as simple and decent a set of basic values as they themselves.

The Plain mother is always the center of her children's world. In most large families, she helps teach them the value of teamwork and makes certain that even the smallest of her offspring is assigned a few chores. A boy of five might carry in chips of wood for the fire; a young girl might be expected to help her older sisters put away kitchen utensils or fold linen. As the children grow older they are expected to learn the skills which one day will enable them to work in the community — the girls will become skilled housekeepers and mothers; the boys will become hardworking, responsible farmers.

Except for the men's wide-brimmed black hats and the families' shoes, most women make all the clothing for the family. On Sundays, when the family wears its "Sunday best," the girls look especially fresh and pretty in their starched prayer bonnets tied with a floppy bow under the chin and their gayly colored dresses of "whipped cream" texture covered by white organdy aprons. In cooler weather they wear long black shawls which fall the entire length of their dresses. The boys' dress is so similar to the men that when one views them from the rear they seem almost a comic miniature of their elders.

By tradition, the husband is the head of the family. Very few disagreements arise between the Plain husband and wife. He uses her as a sounding board, and whether she agrees or not, he makes all the decisions. In our society where women are becoming emancipated, this may well seem unjust, but the Plain People have maintained many traditions the rest of society has either questioned or abandoned. One need not praise or agree with them all.

Divorce is unheard of in their communities.

The women keep busy with home chores and children while the men may work twelve hours a day in the fields.

The Plain People are able to relax easily and look forward to the Sunday preaching service, which is the social event of the week. Whole families congregate outside on benches in the summer months and in barns in colder weather, chatting and joking with one another, often making it a day-long gathering.

When Plain folk buy anything new it is quite an event, especially for the children, who except for their one Sunday outfit, live in hand-me-downs all their young lives. Umbrellas are one of the few items that these people don't make themselves.

I watched a little girl who had just been given her first umbrella. Her parents chose for her not the usual pretty, flimsy children's style, but a full-sized black umbrella. The little girl stood in the yard opening and closing it and admiring the shiny black curved handle. Smiling to herself she hooked the handle over her forearm and paraded along the path, opening it and holding it over her head. I couldn't help being amused at the sight of her in the brilliant sunshine, so eager for a few drops of rain to "christen" her huge umbrella.

Friday night before Sunday preaching service is an especially busy time for the women. The service, plus the traveling, often takes most of the day, and there is no time to prepare the meals. Thus, to enjoy their Sunday, all the girls pitch in on Friday night to help their mothers cook the food needed for the weekend. Flour-covered hands with sleeves rolled above the elbows knead the great mounds of dough for the pies and pastries. Apples are pared, cream whipped, batter mixed, and meat stewed amidst much laughter and chatter.

When school is out and the farm chores are done, I always find the children playing in and around the barns and outbuildings. Although they have very few toys they don't seem to be lonely, and who would be with half a dozen brothers and sisters to keep one company. Off they wander, holding a toddler's hand, down to the pond to poke among the reeds in search of a frog or two. Then, in a flash they're running like deer to the hill-top where they flop down in an exhausted giggling heap.

Unlike our mobile society, where the family unit is often separated by several hundred miles, the Plain families stay very close to one another. In fact, grandparents live in the same house with the oldest married son. This arrangement is easily managed because the people tend to build oversized homes and they simply add rooms as the family grows in size. When the grandparents retire, they usually add a few more rooms onto the house which become comfortable quarters for them. Since the grandfather has been used to a full work day, he busies himself with light chores around the farm and becomes a companion to the smaller children.

Among the Plain People everyone seems to have a hobby. A woman may bake individually-decorated cookies at Christmas time, or she may spend what little spare time she has painting dishes. There is a Mennonite man who cuts daily news items from the paper. Every item, from births, deaths, and marriages, to farming, industry, and weather, have been placed in their categories. He has completed a file of all the events in the Lancaster area for the past forty years and has recently donated it to the Mennonite Information Center, where it is being kept up to date.

An old Amish man who lives in a tiny village near Morgantown makes little wooden barnyard figures. With only one arm and a foot-pedal-driven lathe, he shapes these quaint and sturdy toys and paints them in eye-catching colors for the children. Many visitors come to the shop and with each purchase of several dollars he always adds a free painted figure for the child. With his long white beard and small bent figure, the old toymaker looks like a character right out of a children's illustrated book of fairy tales.

Christmas to the Plain People is mainly a celebration of the birthday of Christ. They do not have Christmas trees nor do they teach their children to believe in the legend of Santa Claus. However they do exchange gifts, which in keeping with their thrifty natures, are often home made and always practical. Lizzie Zook's store is a popular place at Christmas time where the Plain folk like to browse and buy assorted knick-knacks to give as inexpensive gifts.

On Christmas Day the opening of the gifts is a great event for the whole family. Lots are drawn to see who opens his or her present first. This goes on until the very last package has been opened and admired by everyone. The buildup of suspense for the last person must be almost unbearable. The whole episode is savored for many days afterward as an exciting and wonderful occasion.

Although the Plain folk send commercial Christmas cards to their "English" friends, the children make their own. They draw pictures and write little poems on pieces of paper, fold them like regular cards, and give them to family members.

While "English" people have one Christmas dinner per year, these folks give five or six, beginning in late November and ending on January first. Their immediate family plus many friends attend, and therefore a great quantity of food is needed. The women go all out with the traditional dishes and make a special effort to bake a large variety of pies, cakes, cookies and candies.

At this time of year the houses are not decorated with the commercial Yule trimmings. Instead, tiny branches are cut from pine trees, twisted into circular nest-like shapes, and a tiny candle placed in the center. These candle wreaths are used to decorate the dinner table, mantle, and window-sills around the house. After the guests have all arrived the little candles are lit. Combined with the soft lamplight the whole scene is like a fairytale setting. The shadows dance in tune to the flickering lights. The adults and children, dressed in their old world garb, lend to the scene the quality of a Rembrandt painting come to life.

When the voices of children are heard
on the green
And laughing is heard on the hill,
My heart is at rest within my breast
And everything else is still.

William Blake

Oh for boyhood's painless play,
Sleep that wakes in laughing day,
Health that mocks the Doctor's rules,
Knowledge never learned in schools.

John Greenleaf Whittier

If the day and the night are such that
you meet them with joy,
and life emits a fragrance like flowers
and sweet-scented herbs,
is more elastic, more starry,
more immortal — that is your success.

Henry David Thoreau

*The little ones leaped and shouted and laughed
And all the hills echoed.*

William Blake

God forbid that I should go to any heaven in which there are no horses.

Robert Bontine Cunninghame Graham

Upon the island of cheese grows
great plenty of corn.
the ears of which produce
loaves of bread, ready made.
Ralph Erich Rashe

The curfew tolls the knell of parting day,
The lowing herd winds slowly o'er the lea,
The plowman homeward plods his weary way,
And leaves the world to darkness and to me.

Thomas Gray

*The beauty of the old-fashioned
blacksmith was that when you brought
him your horse to be shod
he didn't think of forty other things
that ought to be done to it.*
Sunshine Magazine

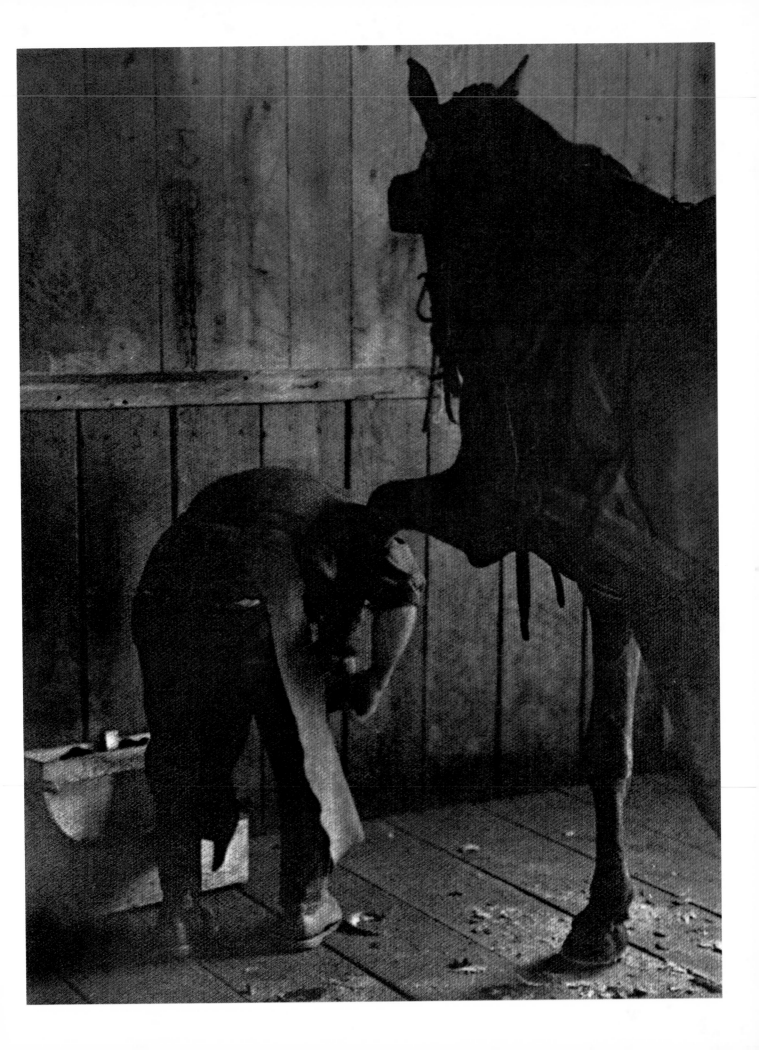

No race can prosper until it learns
that there is as much dignity
in tilling a field as in writing a poem.
Booker Taliaferro Washington

Let us, then, be up and doing,
With a heart for any fate;
Still achieving, still pursuing,
Learn to labor and to wait.

From "A Psalm of Life"
Longfellow

The fields fall southward,
    abrupt and broken,
To the low last edge of the
    long lone land.
If a step should sound or
    a word be spoken,
Would a ghost not rise
    at the strange guest's land?

Algernon Charles Swinburne

Heap high the farmer's wintry hoard!
Heap high the golden corn!
No richer gift has Autumn poured
From out her lavish horn!

John Greenleaf Whittier

The year's at the spring
And day's at the morn;
Morning's at seven;
The hillside's dew-pearled;
The lark's on the wing;
The snail's on the thorn:
God's in his heaven -
All's right with the world.

Robert Browning

No man is born into the world
*   whose work*
Is not born with him; there is
*   always work*
And tools to work withal, for those
*   who will;*
And blessed are the horny hands
*   of toil.*

          James Russell Lowell

That man lives happy and in command
of himself who from day to day
can say, I have lived.
Whether clouds obscure or the sun
illumines the following day,
that which is past is beyond recall.

Horace

Here in an empty manger
Are the ghosts of yesterday,
Where a young and robust farmer
Laid down the tools of his trade.

A lonely scene is this
The tools and animals gone
With the noise and bustle quelled at last
The manger is empty and forlorn.

Beverley Stastny

The sky was pompously playing neighbor
To the unstirring treetops, while the
    distance
Was clamorous with the exchange
Of long-drawn clarion calls of roosters.

Boris Pasternak

The sun, keeping its promise without deception,
Had penetrated early in the morning.

Boris Pasternak

The day is done, and darkness
Falls from the wings of night,
As a feather is wafted homeward
From an eagle in his flight.

Henry Wadsworth Longfellow

Far from the madding crowd's ignoble strife,
Their sober wishes never learned to stray;
Along the cool sequester'd vale of life
They kept the noiseless tenor of their way.

Thomas Gray

The Plain people do not indulge in movies, the theatre, or other "English" forms of entertainment, and the Plain mother is always looking for ways to keep the family amused at home. They are fond of inviting friends for dinner and one novel form of entertainment is to present the guests with a "Mystery Menu." This might read "Asparagus" but the guest will be served lamb chops. Or after asking for carrots the guest might be given a knife and fork. All the food served must be eaten, and one guest who was a school teacher, ended up with six cups in front of him and a very odd assortment of food as well.

The women spend so much time at home that they must set aside a few hours away from the household chores. During "Sister's Day," the women who have pre-school children bundle them into the buggies and drive off, singing away at the tops of their voices. When they arrive at their neighbor's home the children run out to play while the women take out their sewing or knitting and sit down to spend a day together. They all seem to talk at once and sound a little like the workers at the "Tower of Babel."

Most women, especially young girls, like to enhance their appearance in one way or another, and the Plain girls are no exception. But because their faith frowns upon the use of any form of artifice such as makeup or jewelry, they satisfy this urge in the only acceptable way; by wearing glasses. The old saying, "Men never make passes at girls who wear glasses" doesn't seem to worry these girls at all. To see so many young, healthy women wearing spectacles, one would think that there was an inherited sight defect among these people. Obviously some do need them, but several optometrists in the nearby towns do a very brisk business fitting girls who have perfect 20/20 vision, with frames filled with plain glass.

One girl owns two pair — a fancy one, which has one rhinestone on each side of the frame and is worn when she goes out — and a second pair which is very plain and is used at home. The former is considered quite daring in style and therefore all the more enjoyable.

Although the use of perfumes and cosmetics are frowned upon, these people make up for it by using the most highly scented bath soaps and after-shave lotions they can find. The peddlers who include these items in their wares do a profitable business in the Plain communities.

I once went to visit a Plain friend. As I drove along the road I noticed one of his young daughters carrying a package with the name of a large discount department store printed on the side. I stopped and gave her a ride to the house. As we chatted I asked her what was in the package but she wouldn't tell me. She ran upstairs with this mysterious parcel and I thought no more about it.

Then a few weeks later while on another visit to the family, the girl came to me and explained that she would like me to take a picture of her in "Gay" clothes. She confessed that the parcel had contained a modern dress for the occasion. She had also recently bought some earrings, face powder, and even a pair of high-heeled shoes in which she couldn't walk properly. She said she had always wanted to see how she would look dressed in modern clothes, and told me that she often went up into the attic to dress in these things just for fun.

The old saying, "Cleanliness is next to Godliness" must have originally been coined by a Plain housewife.

I had set up my camera on a dirt and gravel back road near an Amish farmhouse in the hope of getting a picture of a buggy as it came over a hill. A few minutes later along came a typical black buggy which I photographed.

As soon as the buggy had gone, a woman came out of a farmhouse and began to sweep the road! I watched in fascination as she bent to pick up a dead leaf here and a broken twig there. Then after she had removed all trace of the buggy wheels with her broom, she bent again and with her hands smoothed the gravel evenly over the dirt road. Plain women who behave in this exaggerated manner are often called "crazy-clean" by their neighbors.

The Chalk Board is found in any Plain home. On it is written the daily schedule for the entire family. Little reminders are jotted down, such as "Visit grandma today," or "Practice singing the hymns," and so on. This board is also seen in the blacksmiths' shops, the dairies and the other places of business. Busy with a variety of chores in distant corners of the fields, barns and sheds, they find that without telephones the best way to keep in touch with one another in an orderly fashion is with the Chalk Board.

Another means of communication is the "Grapevine Telegraph." I was taking pictures in a barn one night when a man rode hurriedly up to the farmhouse. The farmer came to the door and after a brief exchange the visitor quickly rode off down the road toward a neighboring farm. I found out later that this mysterious night rider was relaying news of the death of a man who lived twenty miles away. By morning the whole area would have received the news.

Obedience plays an integral part in the lives of the people.

Obedience to the word of God through the scriptures, and above all, the Ten Commandments. Although the Bible is the symbol of their religion they do not study nor make any effort to understand it. Because of their Swiss-German ancestry, they feel duty bound to read their Bible in "High German." But this language is so far removed from their own mixed rural dialects, that they find it almost impossible to comprehend.

The Plain religion has one of the simplest forms of worship in the Christian world for their services and places of worship lack the superficial trappings of some other faiths. They believe that no matter where they choose to hold preaching service, be it in a simple church, a neighbor's home, a barn, or even a garage, the important thing is that God hears their prayers and is with them always.

At a Plain wedding, although beautiful and ancient hymns are sung, no wedding ring, banks of flowers, or chiming bells are used; yet in its simplicity and purity it is a most delightful and moving ceremony.

How unlike "English" weddings where the expense so often exceeds the family's means. And where, in some cases, the real beauty and meaning of the marriage vows are obscured by the commercial embellishments of the occasion.

Once a person belonging to the Old Order Amish sect breaks away from the group or "Goes Gay" he is shunned not only by his family but by the whole congregation.

A whole family who are good friends of mine left the Old Order Amish to join the more liberal Beachy Amish sect. The incident which follows illustrates the kind of problems these "Gay" people face in their society.

Eli had bought a pony and needed a bridle for it. He asked me to go into town with him and buy it for him. I entered the store and asked for the harness, whereupon the proprietor who was Old Order Amish, happened to look out of the store window and saw Eli waiting for me. The proprietor asked me if the harness was for Eli and I told him it was. Whereupon the man courteously explained that he wouldn't sell me the harness, because Eli had turned his back on his sect and he must be shunned.

One weekend I visited an elderly Amish couple whose eldest son had left their sect to join one with more liberal attitudes. Because of this change of heart, the son, according to his parents' faith, had to give up the farm which was his birthright, and sell all of the animals and equipment. His parents, following their faith's strict code of ethics, were expected to "shun" or disown their son until he chose to repent and return to the old ways.

As I drove up to the house, I noticed that the familiar black buggy and horse were gone and in its place stood the son's brand new car. No children ran out of the barn to greet me and the whole place seemed empty and bare.

The old couple came out of the house to talk to me, and as we chatted I happened to glance into the barn and was struck by its emptiness. The usually clean, neat, and well-stocked interior was bare of farm paraphernalia. The work animals were gone and even the bales of hay had been sold. All that was left to show for the labor and love of three generations was an old yard broom and pitchfork standing alone in a dark corner. The open door swung back and forth in the wind.

The practice of "shunning" has caused much controversy and dissension among the younger generation, and has been one of the main reasons for many to leave the Old Order Amish sect. Strong common bonds hold these people together and those who break the bonds are strongly condemned.

Sometimes, as with children the world over, a young boy or girl will disagree with the sect's strict teachings and "Go Gay," much to the consternation and disappointment of the parents. I had taken some pictures of a seventeen-year-old girl, and when I arrived at her parents' home to present them as a gift, she mentioned that in a week I wouldn't recognize her.

When she met me at the door, the following weekend she was barely recognizable. Her hair hung loosely down her back, she wore make-up, a wrist watch and a short skirt! When I asked how her mother had taken it, she replied, "Oh, Mom will get over it in time." The last time I saw her she was working and living in a nearby town and was much changed by her new life. I remembered her as a fresh-complexioned, pretty girl with a happy disposition. She now appeared to be very subdued and not the carefree teenager of the previous year. I heard recently that she has returned to her faith. This was accomplished in the traditional manner. She repented at preaching services and was at once welcomed back into the fold.

Although one may hear a Plain husband jokingly chide his wife with a remark such as, "Nothing's more beautiful than a woman working," it is a fact that Plain wives themselves take great pride in a clean orderly household and they work hard to keep it that way. Once I happened to notice some long delicate cobwebs hanging down from a grain-bin in a farmer's barn. As the farmer was an Elder in his sect I knew from experience that he might observe the traditional ban against picture-taking on Plain property. Nevertheless I asked him if I might take a picture of the grain bin. The cobwebs were so interesting with the light hitting them at just the right angle.

Much to my surprise he allowed me to use my camera in the barn, and a week later I went back, with those beautiful three-foot-long cobwebs still in my mind, ready to photograph them. The Elder's wife greeted me at the door with, "Jim, I redd-up the barn for you."

I rushed to the barn and found what I had feared. In her kindhearted effort to please me and present a clean interior for me to photograph, she had cleaned out the barn and "redd-up" my beautiful cobwebs into oblivion!

When fire breaks out on a neighboring farm, everyone for miles around rushes to the scene to help put out the blaze. The volunteer Fire Companies are well in evidence in any rural community and although Plain People don't belong to these organizations, they willingly contribute their time and energies when called upon to do so.

Barn raising is an old custom among the Plain People. Because they believe it runs counter to God's will, Plain barns are not protected by lightning rods. Consequently they are often destroyed by fire. This can represent a major financial loss to the farmer, as commercial insurance is not allowed among the sects.

On a pre-arranged day, men and boys come from miles around to help in the construction of the new barn. The foundation is laid prior to the actual raising so that when the men have divided up into work groups they are able to begin erecting the main timbers and framework.

While the men clamber over the barn's skeleton, the young boys help by carrying nails and tools to their fathers and older brothers. With over one hundred and fifty men on the job, this portion of the building is often completed by noon.

Girls and women from the nearby Plain farms supply the refreshments for the mid-day meal. This lunch is eaten midst a holiday atmosphere, for when these folks get together there is much conversation and laughter. By nightfall the barn is usually finished except for interior work which is done by professional Amish carpenters.

The local barns are two-story structures and are always alive with activity. These "bank barns" are so named because of the earthen ramp that is built on the side of one wall which makes it easier for the farmer to wheel in the farm equipment through a second-story door. This ramp also helps to keep the barn warm in winter. The ground level has a concrete floor where the animals are sheltered. Also here one finds the work shop and the room where the harnesses are mended, oiled, and polished.

The second floor or hayloft is partitioned into sections for feed bins and bales of hay. The gabled ends of the second floor are used to cure tobacco, and as a storage space for farm implements. The two or three families of cats that usually inhabit the barn find a snug home in this warm hideaway.

Nowadays the state hygiene laws require dairies to use standard milking machines. Normally these are run by electric current, but as many Plain farmers do not have electricity, they use gasoline generators. The fresh milk is poured into metal milk cans to await pick-up, and is kept cool by an old simple method. Fresh, cool water from a natural spring nearby is piped into two metal boxes and kept at a certain level. These boxes are housed in a small shed built of bricks.

In the summer months preaching services are held in these large cool buildings. Wooden benches are placed in rows and the men sit on one side and the women and children take their places on the other.

When a baby begins to cry during the service the mother takes him out until he has quieted down, then she rejoins the group.

When the congregation prays, they turn as one man away from the preacher, and face the back of the room. The reason for this custom goes back to the time when the people believed that to pray facing the preacher was to pray to him, rather than to God.

Contrary to popular opinion, the Plain sects are not superstitious. The "Hex" signs have never been a part of their culture and the "meanings" behind the various designs painted on their barns were nurtured by commercial interests with an eye to stimulating the tourist trade.

Though some barns in Allentown and Reading display these designs, the Amish and Mennonites consider them to be merely decorations.

The twentieth century with its mass production and built in obsolescence, has fostered in many of us a certain attitude of carelessness and disrespect for objects, many of which are easy to replace. Any contractor will admit that each time he puts his crew to work on a project, he must buy a complete set of new tools. Through carelessness the tools used on previous jobs are always lost, stolen, or broken. By contrast the Plain People treat their farm tools and equipment of nineteenth century craftsmen, with care. At day's end I've often seen a farmer and his sons carefully clean and polish each tool before putting it in a specially designated place in the barn.

The Plain People, with their characteristically frugal nature, make particularly sturdy tools which, with good care, will last through several lifetimes. So, when a young man marries, among the traditional wedding gifts, are always a few used farm tools which the groom is honored to accept.

Very old and beautiful clocks are familiar objects in Plain homes. In addition to the smaller mantel versions seen around the houses are the large antique grandfather clocks.

The old clockmakers can still be found in Plain communities just as their counterparts are to be seen in the little towns and villages of Europe. By tradition the eldest daughter will one day inherit the clocks; therefore it is her duty to wind them regularly. In the quiet of the evening when the children have gone to bed, all that can be heard is the crackle and hiss of the fire and the steady tick of the house clocks.

These are people of the earth, who regard themselves not as landowners, but as guardians of the land for future generations, and so they love their farms without possessiveness, which in our modern society so often breeds ill-will. They are careful to give back what they take from the land. When a man chops down a tree for winter firewood, he always replaces it so that, in twenty years time, his son too will have use of it.

One day I accompanied a man as he inspected some land he wished to buy. As we stood at the edge of a field, he suddenly bent down and took off his shoes. I stared at him in surprise as he began to walk across the ground. When I asked him what the idea was, he explained that he was able to judge the quality of the soil by doing this, and could tell by the moisture content of the earth whether it would be good for planting crops.

In our competitive society a college education seems to many the key to a successful life. Not so with the Plain sects. Their children are not under pressure to become intellectually superior. The general belief is that an eighth grade education is sufficient to see them through life. If a man can acquire the skill necessary to be among the best farmers in the world, he has attained the highest goal set by the community.

Without the help of modern mechanization and chemical fertilizers, the Plain farmers of Lancaster, Pennsylvania, consistently produce the highest percentage of top quality crops per acre, of any farmers in the country. These people have earned for their community the reputation of being the garden spot of the nation.

There's nothing half so pleasant
as coming home again.
Margaret Elizabeth Sangster

If a man love the labor of his trade,
apart from any question of success or
fame, the gods have called him.

Robert Louis Stevenson

And you shall run and wander
And you shall run and sing
Of brave things and bright things
Beyond the swallow's wing.

Fanny Stearns Davis

And many strokes,
though with a little axe,
Hew down and fell the
hardest-timbered oak.
William Shakespeare

The longest journey is
the journey inward.
Dag Hammarsskjold

The pulse of horses' hoofbeats
On the hard gray asphalt road;
The rumble of the wagon wheels
Now lightened of their load;
A farming man with sinews strained
To hold the horses to his will,
His shirt with honest sweat is stained
As they labor up the hill.

Beverley Stastny

A haze on the far horizon,
The infinite tender sky,
The ripe rich tint of the corn-fields,
And the wild geese sailing high -
And all over upland and lowland
The charm of the golden rod,
Some of us call it Autumn,
And others call it God.

William Herbert Carruth

The wild hawk to the windswept sky,
The deer to the wholesome wold
And the heart of a man to the heart of a maid,
As it was in the days of old.

Rudyard Kipling

*All doors are flung open -
in stable and in cowbarn.*
Boris Pasternak

The body travels more easily than the mind, and until we have limbered up our imagination we continue to think as though we had stayed home. We have not really budged a step until we take up residence in someone else's point of view.

John Erskine

Happy the man, whose wish and care
A few paternal acres bound,
Content to breathe his native air
In his own ground.

Alexander Pope

I watch the green field growing
For reaping folk and sowing,
For harvest-time and mowing,
A sleepy world of streams.

Algernon C. Swinburne

Anyone who has been in the Lancaster area has seen the familiar black horse-drawn buggy full of children swaying around a bend. As it draws away one can see a little child's face peeping from the back window. The sunny smile and friendly wave seem to be irresistible to the average person and so it is with me.

In contrast to the ultra-conservative groups, who, by the edicts of their faith, are not permitted to own automobiles, the Mennonites, Dunkards, and "Beachy" Amish are free to do so. But the cars they drive are acceptable only on condition that they are uniformly black with no frivolous decoration. Some members paint the chrome trim and bumpers black to give an even more subdued appearance. This practice has resulted in the local term, "Black Bumper Amish." Nevertheless, the rumble of wagon wheels and the steady clip-clop of the horses' hooves is a part of Lancaster county. Many Plain folk prefer to use the horse and buggy as their regular means of transport. Therefore they are very dependent on their horses, and these animals are the love of a Plain man's life. The horses used to draw the family buggies are beautiful high-spirited creatures with lines akin to the race-horse. The farm horses are the huge barrel-chested Clydesdales and Belgians with the handsome beauty typical of their breed. Finer judges of horse flesh would be hard to find, and when it comes to buying livestock they drive a hard but fair bargain and enjoy the haggling.

The children adopt all kinds of stray creatures, including foxes, mice, wild birds, raccoons, and even snakes, to keep as pets. A whole family will often go up to the mountains for a picnic. As night falls they sit very quietly and watch the mating and foraging habits of the deer and other wild forest creatures. This pastime is called "Spotting deer."

Although the barns and outbuildings abound with cats of all colors and sizes, each one is considered important and enjoys equal status along with the other pets. One Saturday as I drove up to a farm, I saw six or seven Plain women running across a field with skirts flying and black-stockinged legs moving like pistons. As they are usually on the more dignified side, I thought something really disastrous had happened.

It seems that Emma's cat had leaped into the feed-truck which had just made a delivery at the farm. As the truck made its way toward the next farm, the women tried without success to head it off by cutting across the field.

The truck arrived at the neighboring farm but by the time the women caught up with it the cat had panicked and vanished. By this time about fifteen children had joined in the chase, all calling the cat, while peering into barns and bushes. In the meantime I reached Emma's house, only to be greeted by her daughter who held the vagrant cat in her arms. I was given the job of driving around to pass the word that the "Prodigal" had returned under his own power, and was none the worse after his first experience hitchhiking.

A cheerful characteristic of these Plain People is their love of singing. They take great pleasure in performing together their ancient and beautiful hymns at preaching services and weddings. The tunes of these are similar to medieval chants and are so complicated they often take years to master.

One summer day I visited a family for whom I had done a few favors. Wishing to show their appreciation in some way the whole family sang hymns to me. They had just begun singing when the three "English" children from next-door ran in to join us. They stood there and happily sang along with the other children. Plain People sing as they go about their work in the fields, around the house, and when driving along the winding country roads. A Plain child can't seem to ride in a moving vehicle without bursting into song.

In a Plain home the Sunday guest is urged to follow his host and hostess's example by slipping his shoes off, stretching out on a sofa or easy chair and taking an hour's nap. I was once a guest at the home of a Mennonite family. After dinner as we were relaxing and chatting in the living room while the teenage daughters sang in the kitchen, I noticed that the phone there was off the hook. I mentioned this to my host and he told me that while washing the dishes each Sunday evening, his daughters used that time to sing hymns to a lonely, bed-ridden old "English" woman. The girls had never met this woman but their mother had met her many years before, and knew just how much this contact with others meant to her. The girls' mother would go into the kitchen every now and then with little notes advising them what hymns she thought the old lady might enjoy. Several months later at a social gathering I met the old lady, who was in a wheel-chair. As was her habit she had made a little gift for one of the girls.

For a long time I had wanted to know in advance where the next church services in the area would be held, so that I could photograph a string of buggies driving along a country road. Their services are usually held in a neighbor's home or a barn. And as the arrangements are carried by word of mouth, this was a problem for me because by the time I found their whereabouts, it was too late.

One day while riding along with an Amish friend I mentioned my difficulty. He said, "Jim, all you have to do is look for the increased amount of horse droppings on the road and follow them." Although at first I felt a little like the boy from "Hansel and Gretel," I soon got over it. Since then I have followed this unusual road marker and it has never failed me.

The story behind the Plain term "God's Little Acre" helps illustrate the Plain People's idea of charity. Each family sets aside one acre of land to raise a particular crop. One family might grow corn, another tomatoes, another strawberries and so on.

As a regular project, several girls get together and set out on a "Weeding Frolic," They go from farm to farm watering, weeding, and generally caring for these acres until harvest time. After they harvest the crops, the girls choose a house. Working quickly and efficiently they can and label the produce and distribute it to nearby "English" orphanages.

Not long ago a one-armed peddler who said he was a World War II veteran, went from house to house in the Plain communities of Lancaster for almost a year selling shoe-laces and other odds and ends to the farm women. He seemed to have moved on and no one gave it a thought.

Then one day about a year later he reappeared at the home of an Amish woman named Rachel who had always been exceptionally kind to him. He told her that his other arm would have to be amputated, unless he could raise one thousand dollars for the operation. Rachel gave him sixty-five dollars and passed the word on to her neighbors. They all contributed what they could and it wasn't long until the required amount was reached. Off the man went with promises to write and let these good ladies know the outcome of the operation. When no word came the Plain women's "English" neighbors grew suspicious and contacted the police.

It seems that the one-armed man had used the same story in all the Plain communities, and had made a nice haul to the tune of several thousand dollars.

I happened to mention to Rachel that it was a pretty dirty trick the peddler played on her and the other women; but instead of bearing malice toward the man she said, "I'm not sure he did anything wrong. If I'd refused to give him the money and he'd needed it, then I'd really feel bad."

Outsiders are often amazed at the sight of a Plain farmer sealing an important deal, involving perhaps thousands of dollars, with nothing more substantial than a handshake. This is because they deal mainly among themselves.

A form of "Honor System" is used at the roadside produce-stands. The owners put a box with small change on the stand with the fruit and vegetables. When called away to the fields the "English" customer serves himself and makes change. I asked one farmer whether he had much trouble being short-changed. He answered that surprisingly, the cash nearly always balanced.

The custom of intermarriage among the Plain People plays an important part in keeping the sects together. It has also resulted in a profusion of two dozen or so typical Plain surnames.

For example in one community there might be fifteen Ben Fishers. Therefore when speaking of one in particular they use the wife's Christian name to make the distinction, refer-ring to the man in question as Rebecca's Ben or Sarah's Eli, as the case may be.

Stemming from this abundance of identical names is the custom of labeling an individual with a distinguishing nick-name, usually of a humorous origin. A boy once accidentally poured gravy into his coffee instead of milk. Until the day he died he was known as "Gravy Dan." Ben Yost as a boy was badly injured in a fall from his horse. His leg never healed properly and for the rest of his life he walked with a limp. He was nicknamed "Lame Yost." If a child is crippled he will often be referred to through his mother's name, for example, "Martha's cripple."

If for some reason a Plain farmer has to sell his property, he will never sell to an outsider if he can help it. One case I remember was of an elderly man who had left the Old Order Amish sect.

Although he was moving away to a completely new area he still would not sell his property to an "English" farmer and eventually did sell his farm to a member of his sect so that the land would stay a part of the Plain community.

Often a Plain farmer who would like to expand is prevented from doing so because of the high-priced "English" owned properties bordering his land. The solution for many has been to sell out and move to new areas of the state where the taxes are lower and the tourists rare.

In the past, tourists have sometimes been overeager to capture on film the quaint charm of the Plain communities and the people. Consequently they have taught their children to cover their faces and run away when approached by "Outsiders" with cameras.

I recently witnessed a group of about thirty camera-toting tourists sight a couple of little boys walking over the fields toward their home. The boys saw the tourists at the same moment, and having been taught to keep clear of such people, they began to run away. The tourists gave chase just as the boys disappeared from view over a grassy knoll. When the tourists reached the top of the rise they shouted to one another, "There they are! Come on over this way and head them off." The last I saw was the distant figures of the little boys, who'd had a good headstart, reaching their homeground and disappearing behind the barn.

Another time, I was sitting and chatting with a blacksmith friend of mine while he shod a horse. A car full of tourists stopped just outside his shop. Although he had a large sign which read "No Pictures" they walked in, cameras at the ready. One man picked up a horse shoe and said he wanted to buy it for a souvenir.

Luke agreed to sell it to the man for a dollar if he would wait until he'd finished shoeing the horse. Without bothering to ask permission these people began taking flash-bulb pictures of the whole interior including Luke shoeing the horse. They continued this for a quarter of an hour while the horse became more and more jittery. This didn't make the job easier for Luke who was doing his best to control himself.

When they had finally gone he turned to me with a look of relief and said, "When I tell my wife about this she'll be very proud that I didn't lose my temper."

Although their family life is warm and tightly knit, with many children and grandparents to keep one another company, when I leave a home I have the feeling often that some of the Plain People would like closer contact with and stimulation from the outside world. Driving away down a dirt road at dusk, I often stop and look back into the growing darkness. There a solitary farmhouse stands like an island of light, the soft, warm glow of lanterns steadfastly keeping the house separate from the oncoming night. The atmosphere is so peaceful, yet the isolation so profound one realizes the Plain People are living in such a way that time for them stands still.

*Sometimes when looking deep
into the eyes of a child,
you are conscious of meeting a glance
full of wisdom. The child has known
nothing yet but love and beauty -
all this piled-up world knowledge
you have acquired is unguessed at by
him. And yet you meet this
wonderful look that tells you
in a moment more than all the years
of experience have seemed to teach.*

Hildegarde Hawthorne

With the sunshine on thy face,
Through thy torn brim's jaunty grace;
From my heart I give thee joy —
I was once a barefoot boy!

John Greenleaf Whittier

True friends have no solitary
joy or sorrow.
Channing

Blest, who can unconcern'dly find
Hours, days, and years, slide soft away
In health of body find, peace of mind,
Quiet by day.

Alexander Pope

So lonely 'twas, that God himself
Scarce seemed there to be.
Samuel Taylor Coleridge

My little horse must think it queer
To stop without a farmhouse near
Between the woods and frozen lake
The darkest evening of the year.

He gives his harness bells a shake
To ask if there is some mistake,
The only other sound's the sweep
Of easy wind and downy flake.

Robert Frost

Every child should know a hill,
And the clean joy of running down its
long slope
With the wind in his hair.

Edna Casler Joll

She stood as noble as a tower
Pure of impeachment as the sky,
As much an earth-bloom as the flower;
The slow winds flowed austerely by,
And she was of their harmony.

Arthur Davison Ficke

We grow neither better nor worse
as we get old,
but more like ourselves.
Mary Pemberton Becker

I shall see his toys and his empty chair,
And the horse he used to ride,
And they will speak with a silent speech
Of the little boy that died.

Joshua Davenport Robinson

Children are what the mothers are.
No fondest father's fondest care
Can fashion so the infant heart.

Walter Savage Landor

When I am dead, my dearest,
Sing no sad songs for me;
Plant thou no roses at my head,
Nor shady cypress tree.

Christina Georgina Rossetti

I remember the gleams and glooms that dart
Across the school-boy's brain;
The song and the silence on the heart,
That in part are prophecies, and in part
Are longings wild and vain.
And the voice of that fitful song
Sings on and is never still:
"A boy's will is the wind's will,
And the thoughts of youth are
        long, long thoughts."

John Greenleaf Whittier

Easy, wind!
Go softly here!
She is small
And very dear.

She is young
And cannot say
Words to chase
The wind away.

She is new
To walking, so
Wind, be kind
And gently blow.

On her ruffled head,
On grass and clover,
Easy, wind . . .
She'll tumble over!

Frances M. Frost

I see with inward eye serene
A green and lovely sight,
A quaint old-fashioned pastoral scene
There, in the sun's last light.

A silhouette of man and cart,
Rolling slowly by,
Down a dusty country road,
Under a burnished sky.

Beverley Stastny

Like the dew on the mountain,
Like the foam on the river,
Like the bubble on the fountain,
Thou art gone, and forever!

Sir Walter Scott

Walk along a country lane
Through the summer haze.
Listen to the skylark's song,
Enjoy the golden days.

Swing along a country road
When all the world seems new,
Gaze up at the cotton clouds
Pinned to a canvas of blue.

A hidden nook I'm seeking,
A green and shady place,
Where I can rest and be at peace
In nature's soft embrace.

Beverley Stastny

Church bells at evening, wafted far
To one who stands upon a hill
And gazes toward the sunset spire
Through distance luminous and still,

Are as a seal of peace upon
His heart, a laying of God's hand
Upon him in the evening glow
Above the quiet land.

Adelaide Love

*The mother's face and voice
are the first conscious objects as the
infant soul unfolds,
and she soon comes to stand in
the very place of God with her child.*
Granville Stanley Hall

The text for this book was set in Press
Roman and the color separations
and printing were done by
Vernon Martin Associates, Inc.
Lancaster, Pennsylvania.
The first edition of this
volume consisted of
five thousand
copies.